LIVING LIFE AS A
GODLY
CHAMPION

DR. H. WESLEY DYKES JR.

ARPress
ILLUMINATING IDEAS.
EMPOWERING VOICES

ARPress

45 Dan Road Suite 5
Canton, MA 02021

Hotline: 1(888) 821-0229
Fax: 1(508) 545-7580

Ordering Information:

Quantity sales. Special discounts are available on quantity purchases by corporations, associations, and others. For details, contact the publisher at the address above.

Printed in the United States of America.

ISBN-13:   Softcover   979-8-89389-592-6
              eBook   979-8-89389-593-3

Library of Congress Control Number: 2024921084

F O R E W O R D

From the moment my husband expressed to me that he was led by God to write a book, I was so happy for him. Both my husband and I hold strong to our faith, and there is nothing more exciting than being able to share this book with you. Wesley is full of biblical knowledge and has a strong passion for Christ. *Living Life as a Godly Champion* is a book written about being a godly leader, trusting, loving, and following God with all your heart, mind, and soul. Wesley has always strived to live his life as an effective leader for the glory of Jesus Christ. His journey began at an incredibly young age from his close-knit family who always encouraged him to do his best in life and live a life after our heavenly father. Everything that he has done, from playing Little League Baseball to playing football throughout middle school, high school, and college, Wesley was always building up, encouraging, and pushing people to strive to do their best. He had a dream of becoming a physical therapist so he could help others, but God had other plans for him. God was pushing him to become a physician; He knew that my husband had so much more to offer. Wesley fought this feeling repeatedly as that was not his dream. God has a funny way of making you do something that you do not want or think you can do. Today Wesley is a successful sports medicine physician and flight surgeon serving in the United States Air Force for over twenty years. I am so proud of you, honey, and could not be prouder to be your wife. I love you wholeheartedly. Be blessed, godly champions!

Mrs. Misti Dykes

INTRODUCTION

꘎ ꘎

G od gave me the concept of "godly champion" several years ago and directed me to write this book. Initially I thought that the motivating factor behind writing this book was to leave a reminder of the many discussions held and lessons taught to my children over the years. However, in time the Lord made it clear to me that this book was also meant to be shared with His chosen people. A champion, as defined by Merriam-Webster dictionary, is *"one who shows marked superiority."* As children of the almighty God, we are markedly superior because of the acceptance, belief, and faith in our Lord Jesus Christ. God repeatedly states throughout the Bible that He would never leave us nor forsake us. God ensures the victory for us in every circumstance, situation, challenge, or obstacle. He works out everything for our good because we love Him and are called according to His purpose (Romans 8:28). This is what we can expect from God in our godly champion partnership. What God expects or demands from us is our love, worship, obedience, trust, and devotion to Him only. Being a champion in any regard requires diligent work. Therefore, godly champions must commit to praying continually, reading and studying the Bible consistently, worshiping Him daily, and trusting and obeying Him always. We as God's children represent Him every second of the day, whether we are in the confines of our homes or at a public/corporate venue. He expects us to represent Him honorably, diligently, zealously, courageously, and with great swag. That's right, swag! I wholeheartedly believe God wants us to represent Him proudly with a colorful, spirited style. Although we encounter trials, tribulations, and setbacks, we adapt, adjust, and overcome all obstacles because of the strength and grit afforded to us by the indwelling Holy Spirit. This embodies the persona of a godly champion. We are victorious!

THE ESSENTIALS OF A GODLY CHAMPION

A godly champion (GC) is a man, woman, boy, or girl whose heart is solely dedicated unto God and His will, purpose, and plan for his/her life and family. Godly champions are not perfect people but have committed their lives to serve the Lord (as exemplified by Joshua in the Bible). They are God's elect, His chosen people, royal priesthood who strap on spiritual armor every day and conquer challenges of the flesh, world, and Satan with relentless tenacity. Godly champions are God's ultimate warriors who look like you and me. They are represented by every race, creed, ethnicity, nationality, and socioeconomic background. They realize their measure of success is not defined or determined by position, power, or worldly possessions amassed but defined or determined by the achievement of God's purpose, plan, and will for their lives. Although mistakes, poor decisions, or bad choices may be made, it is well known that with confession and repentance to our heavenly father with a contrite heart and willingness to heed correction, a fortuitous outcome can be yielded. However, it is important to note that unfavorable consequences may ensue if ill-advised decisions or mistakes give way to sinful acts. God is immune to sin, and He does not tolerate sin from us. Therefore, the ensuing consequences potentially experienced are a result of God's response to our commission of sin, which is intended to discipline us because He loves us and desires the very best for us.

GCs are passionate servant leaders consistent in judgment and character, seeking to serve God with great confidence and humility. Godly champions live their lives intentionally with great boldness and courage and are fueled to serve by the strength of their everlasting faith, peace, passion, and hope in almighty God. It is understood that the god of this universe has given them abundant favor, love, grace, and mercy to accomplish His will for their lives for which they were called. GCs have sought God to understand the gifts, talents, and skills that He has blessed them with to use for His glory. They work hard, sharpening their crafts to honor God shamelessly and relentlessly. In spite of their mistakes made in the past, GCs know that they've been redeemed by the priceless blood of Jesus Christ shed on the cross, and thus, they live in profound freedom from judgment and condemnation. They readily love others and give generously without fail. They are humble and kind yet bold and courageous. They are not weak doormats by any means. The power of God's touch exudes from them as they live and operate in their calling. GCs understand that the way they live their lives is an act of worship unto God and potentially an impactful statement to those in the world who may be lost spiritually. Every word spoken, every action and reaction performed should reflect God's glory. However, their lives are not perfect. At times, they make mistakes, miss the mark, and are knocked down; however, they get back up because they are held firmly by the righteous right hand of God. They intentionally strive daily to represent God in the best light possible like true ambassadors of Christ. They have come to the realization that the true measure of our success is contingent upon their willingness to fulfill the purpose, plan, and will of God for which they were created. The biblical standards, decrees, directives, and commands set forth by almighty God are the very foundation from which decisions are made and actions performed. GCs realize that all will go well for them if we make seeking God the number-one priority in every facet of our lives and abide by His laws, commands, directives, decrees, and standards.

God desires premium quality of the hearts of His chosen people. He desires that we put forth our best in every situation, circumstance, or condition that we're involved in because we invariably represent Him. Our lives are to be lived as daily acts of worship unto Him. God uses us as signaling mirrors. As we live our lives in a pleasing manner unto God, His radiant glory reflects off us to be seen by the world for the advancement of His kingdom on earth.

Colossians 3:23–24 commands us to work at whatever we do with all our heart, working for the Lord to glorify Him, not to appease people. We are to strive to seek God's approval first and foremost in everything that we do so that life may go well for us. Promotion for us comes from God, not from man; however, He may opt to use man as a vessel through which His blessings flow. Thus, if we commit ourselves to making God the top priority in our lives and focus our attention and efforts on pleasing Him above everything else, then all other things will fall into place. As a result, we will not have to concern ourselves with jumping through hoops trying to please different people to curry favor or gain their approval. We must always do what is right regardless of the situation or what's at stake. We must not compromise our morals and ethics to appease a boss, a spouse, relatives, parents, friends, loved ones, teachers, coaches, or teammates. It is He who has created and purposed us to fulfill His will, plan, and mission to impact the world for Him. Therefore, it would behoove us to accomplish every task, assignment, or responsibility with an unrelenting effort, regardless of the level of importance, to gratify our Lord.

Winning isn't what makes a GC notable. A noteworthy godly champion knows how to enjoy the high spirit of a victory and understands that a defeat or a failure isn't final nor is he/she defined by his/her defeats or failures. It's all about attaining God's perspective on the matters of life and how He sees everything, win or lose. God created us to win the war of life, although we may lose some battles. Victory is final and resides with God. Therefore, a GC walks with confidence in all situations knowing that the power and peace of God reside in his/her heart and that no weapon formed against him/her will prosper (Isaiah 54:17).

My participation in team sports has played an integral role in my growth, development, and maturity as a boy, man of God, and godly champion. I passionately love sports and have learned so many lessons about life through playing sports. I began playing sports at five years old when my mother signed me up for baseball, and I finished my organized competitive sports career after playing one year of college football. I participated in baseball, football, and ran track throughout my athletic career before calling it quits and pursuing a career in medicine. I had the blessings of being on teams with both winning and losing records as well as championship teams. I gleaned pearls of wisdom by playing on each one of those teams. However, the distinguishing characteristic of the championship teams, aside from remarkable athletic talent, is that the positive, winning attitude and heart of a champion spirit personified by the head coach and coaching staff permeated throughout the team. Athletes and fans respect and admire good, positive, winning head coaches. They tend to ascertain what makes those winning coaches special and how can they learn and model those winning attributes or characteristics. GC team, God is our epitomical, spiritual-championship-winning head coach, and we are His chosen team. He expects us to adopt and reflect His championship heart, spirit, and attitude. This can be accomplished by devoting ourselves to His championship game plan. What is God's game plan for our success? Reading and studying the Bible, praying to Him, worshiping Him, trusting and obeying Him, and by ascertaining then executing His excellent purpose, plan, and will for our lives. When we adopt the attributes of God's character (i.e., love, mercy, forgiveness, patience) and allow them to permeate our hearts as well as routinely demonstrate His character to the rest of the world for His sake, then we exhibit the championship DNA instilled in us by almighty God at the time of our creation. Luke 6:45 and Matthew 12:35 essentially tells us that a good person displays good things out of the good stored up in his/her heart. Likewise, an evil person displays evil things out of the evil stored up in his/her heart. Out of the overflow of the heart the mouth speaks." In the same vein, Matt 7:15 states that "a good tree cannot bear bad fruit and a bad tree cannot bear good fruit. Each tree will be recognized by the fruit that it bears." Contextually, this passage of Scripture means that we are constantly being judged by our actions, reactions, attitudes, speech, and nonverbal behavior such as facial expressions. These characteristics can be labeled as "displayed fruit," so to speak. The fruit displayed is a direct reflection of contentment in our hearts that speaks to our character. Ideally, our character should mirror that of our Lord and Savior Jesus Christ. Therefore, the fruit that we ("trees") should display should closely resemble the fruit of the Holy Spirit. The fruits of the Holy Spirit are peace, patience, gentleness, goodness, kindness, love, faithfulness, joy, and self-control (Galatians 5:22) as well as humility and compassion. By displaying this "good fruit," we can make a profound impact on the world's population for our God and advance His kingdom on earth.

We must be careful how we conduct ourselves and how we walk throughout life, for we're God's elect, His chosen, holy people. We're called to be *light* in the world (Ephesians 5:8) to illuminate the darkness of this world. We're the salt of the earth so that we can make an indelible impact on those our Lord allows to cross our path. We're God's arms and legs in the world to accomplish His great purpose, plan, and will. We were bought at a price; thus, we are not our own (1 Corinthians 6:19–20, 7:23). Jesus laid down His life for us so that we may be reconciled with God and experience everlasting love and life. We belong to God, and it is He who works in us and through us to will and act according to His good purpose (Philippians 2:13).

To reflect God's glory, it is imperative that we conduct ourselves in a manner that is worthy of spreading the gospel of Jesus Christ (Philippians 1:27) and live a life worthy of the calling and purpose that we have received from God (Ephesians 4:1). This is essential because the world is watching, and it is incumbent upon us to get God's message of love, hope, faith, peace, and redemption to them. We have been created to fulfill God's perfect purpose, plan, and will for our lives, and each of us has been given grace apportioned by Christ to accomplish our God-given calling (Ephesians 4:7). There are essential attributes that we as GCs must demonstrate routinely: humility, love, peace, forgiveness, generosity, and faith.

The heart is the foundational epicenter for a person's character and, thus, reflects the person. Proverbs 4:23 and 23:7 (KJV) states, "For as a man thinketh in his heart, so is he." Character is extremely important to the Lord. Jesus, noted in Matthew 23:25–26 and Luke 11:39–40, excoriated the Pharisees for being very hypocritical. They were walking around pompously professing to be teachers of God's law to the Jews, but in their hearts, as Jesus Christ revealed, they were full of greed and wickedness. He admonished them to first clean their hearts, then the righteous, outward expression of the heart would be truly effective. He metaphorically said this by stating, "First clean the inside of the cup and dish, and then the outside will also be clean." Paul wrote to the Colossians, strongly admonishing them to set their hearts on things above where Christ is seated at the right hand of God (Colossians 3:1). In essence, Paul is saying, "Align your focus and character with that of God's." Everything and in everything is all about Him!

Our speech and behavior are reflective of the content of our hearts. We have to be mindful of how we verbally communicate with people so that our representation of Christ isn't tainted or poorly received and, thus, possibly disqualify us from reaching them for God. It is important for us to remember that our speech and behavior must always be honorable so that God may be glorified. Colossians 3:17 reminds us that "whatever we do, whether in word or deed, do it all in the name of the Lord Jesus Christ." Ephesians 4:25, 29 tells us that we must "speak truthfully to one and other and not to allow any unwholesome talk to come out of our mouths but only that which encourages and builds others up." Further, Ephesians 5:4 instructs us to be "void of obscenity, foolish talk, and coarse joking." Proverbs 4:24 encourages us to "put away perversity from your mouths and to keep corrupt talk far from your lips." Psalm 34:13 admonishes us to "keep our tongues from evil and our lips from speaking lies." Colossians 3:8 charges us to "rid ourselves of slander and filthy language." Lastly, "our conversations should always be full of grace, seasoned with salt, so that we may know how to answer everyone" (Colossians 4:6). What I'm trying to emphasize here is if we are to reflect the heart of God and Jesus Christ to be His beacon of light to the masses, we must always be mindful of what comes out of our mouths and the tone and tenor by which it's delivered.

I would be totally remiss if I did not make mention of the aspect of fear in light of being a godly champion. Fear is a common human emotional response to a daunting or troubling situation(s). However, simply stated, faith and fear cannot coexist; they are mutually exclusive. Here are some rudimentary but salient points about fear and faith:

- Our level of faith in God is predicated on the degree of love, trust, and belief/obedience that we possess for Him.
- With great faith comes great favor. Great favor = great blessings. With small faith comes small favor. Small favor = small blessings.
- One sure way great faith is developed is through trials, tribulations, and challenges we face and endure as we mature in God's ordained walk while navigating the precarious maze of life. The beautiful thing is that our heavenly father knows the appropriate degree of difficulty and timing of the rigors we face to elicit His

desired change to effectively shape our lives, resulting in the newly graduated level of faith accomplished. This cycle perpetuates throughout our lives until we're called home to be with Him.

- Fear is a tool used by Satan to impair, paralyze, derail, detour, and/or shipwreck us and to preclude us from accomplishing our God's perfect plan, purpose, and will for our lives. The late Martin Luther said, "God and the devil take opposite tactics regarding fear. The Lord first allows us to become afraid, that he might relieve our fears, and comfort us. The devil, on the other hand, first makes us feel secure in our pride and sins, that we might later be overwhelmed with fear and despair."

- God didn't give us a spirit of fear (2 Timothy 1:7).

- Faith in God inherently entails the promises of God (Isaiah 41:8–15, 43:1–5).

- God desires for us to be bold, strong, and courageous (Joshua 1:1–9) because that is the way He created us along with humility, kindness, and compassion.

- Fear will cripple or paralyze us and prevent us from reaching our God-given goals and endeavors.

Author Vance K. Jackson teaches this by saying "God wants us to move forward in your purpose, plan, and destiny. For we walk by faith and not by sight. God has not given us a spirit of timidity; therefore, as His children, we do not walk in fear; we walk in power, love, and sound mind." He also stated that "when you're in a constant state of being fearful, our decisions and actions are double minded and unstable." James 1:8 (KJV) states, "A double minded man is unstable in all his ways." Fear leads to instability. Instability leads to spiritual impairment resulting in spiritual unproductivity. I know at times that fear can be gripping in the face of perceived formidable challenges; however, we are expected to walk by faith and not by sight.

- As stated earlier, fear and faith cannot coexist; they are mutually exclusive (like Ford and Chevrolet automobiles, Samsung and Apple electronics, and Nikon and Canon cameras). Their parts are not interchangeable. Fear perpetuated is bondage, a form of slavery that can and will have you walking around in circles much like the Israelites did when they were in the wilderness for forty years. However, unflappable faith emboldens you. It pushes you to the margins of your comfort zone to achieve new heights and to soar to endless bounds. Fear subtracts, faith adds. Unchecked fear is catabolic, unfettered faith is anabolic. Dwelling on fear is exhaustive. It robs you of your energy, strips you of joy, and in the end, it leaves you in a state of physical, emotional, mental, and spiritual distress. Focusing on faith inspires energy; it is spiritually exhilarating and engenders hope. There is an inverse relationship that exists between fear and faith, meaning if there is an abundance of one, then there's a paucity of the other. As your faith abounds in God, you increase in power, strength, and courage, and consequently, your fearfulness decreases. As you increase in fear, you increase in anxiety, stress, and weakness, resulting in detrimental health effects. Unwavering faith is the engine that drives you to victorious living. Fear allowed to fester stumps spiritual growth and can result in a shipwrecked destiny. God created us to be champions for Him, to succeed according to His plan and by His standards, not to be dominated or mastered by fear. God has given power to us afforded by the Holy Spirit to conquer all fears. 2 Peter 1:3 informs us that "His divine power has given us everything we need for a godly life through our knowledge of him who called us by his own glory and goodness." Romans 8:37 proclaims, "In all things we are more than conquerors through Him who loved us."

Tenents of a Godly Champion

Love the Lord your God with All Your Heart, Soul, Mind, and Strength

This command speaks to the core of our essential foundational belief and existence. In order for us to glorify God, fulfilling our God-given purposes, we must first love God with all our hearts, souls, minds, and strength. Then we have to trust and obey Him. Here are some scriptures that support this tenant:

- Love the Lord your God and keep His requirements, His decrees, His laws, and commands always (Deuteronomy 11:1, 13).
- Love the Lord your God with all your heart, soul, and strength (Deuteronomy 6:5).
- Fear the Lord your God, walk in obedience to Him, love Him, serve the Lord your God with all your heart and with all your soul, and observe the Lord's commands and decrees (Deuteronomy 10:12).

- Love the Lord God and serve Him with all your heart and soul (Deuteronomy 11:13).
- Love the Lord your God, walk in obedience to Him, and hold fast to Him (Deuteronomy 11:22, 19:9).
- Be very careful to keep that commandment and those laws: to love God, obey Him, keep His commands, hold fast to Him, and serve Him with all your heart and soul (Joshua 22:5, 23:11).
- Love your God, listen to His voice, and hold fast to Him. For the Lord is your life, and He will give you many years in the land He swore to your fathers (Deuteronomy 30:16).
- Love your God, walk in obedience to Him, and keep His commands, decrees, and laws. Then you will live and increase, and the Lord your God will bless you in the land you're entering to possess (Deuteronomy 30:16).
- Love the Lord your God with all your heart, all your soul, and all your mind (Matthew 22:37).

Do Everything with a Spirit of Excellence/an Excellent Spirit

This is profoundly important to exemplify. This speaks to how we should conduct our behavior in every circumstance or situation (no matter how big or small). As godly champions, we should always approach every task, chore, assignment, delegation, task order, or responsibility with the mindset that we will render a 100-percent effort or top-notch performance in the accomplishment of whatever is bestowed upon us. When we operate with an excellent spirit, we prolifically praise, honor, and glorify our heavenly father, reveal His spirit, and project His image onto others. This indeed is a proud act of worship unto our God that undoubtedly pleases Him.

Colossians 3:23–24 states, "Whatever you do, work with all your heart, as working for the Lord, not to men, since you know that you will receive an inheritance from the Lord as reward."

This scripture is applicable to every functional activity that we perform. No matter how menial or trivial the task. I love this scripture because it highlights the important fact that in everything that we do, our primary focus should be to honor and please God and that He will appropriately reward our performance in His timing. So if we are cooking, cleaning, working, exercising, teaching, parenting, praying, or worshiping, we are to give it our best effort with regard to our given state or condition. Those times when we are functioning or operating suboptimally due to illness, fatigue, exhaustion, etc., we are expected to give maximum effort for that given state although it may not be our overall best. So many times I've heard people say, "I'm not doing that because I don't get paid enough," or "They do not pay me enough to work that hard or perform a certain task or tasks." This, in my opinion, is a travesty. Proverbs 18:9 states, "One who is slack in his work is brother to him who destroys." Now, I want to preface my ensuing thoughts by first saying this: I am fundamentally opposed to employers exploiting their employees by instructing them to perform unscrupulous tasks or functions well beyond the scope of their agreed-upon or contracted position description or giving them compensation disproportionate to an inordinate amount of work performed, thus, violating a pre-employment agreement/contract. Regardless of the circumstance or circumstances, I implore you not to compromise your morals, values and/or ethics. I know that it can be an ominous feeling when your boss or supervisor is ordering, instructing, or asking you to do something contradictory to your ethos or fundamental beliefs, core values, and/or God's word, especially if you are the proverbial breadwinner or are working in your dream job. However, despite the level of difficulty, our prevailing thought must be that we are children of the almighty God and, first and foremost, work for Him and uphold His standards. We are accountable to Him ultimately, and all our actions will be judged accordingly. Therefore, if your job or position is contingent upon you performing a deed that obviously is not right legally, morally, or ethically, it would be best for you by God's standards that you do not perform the deed or task and trust Him for the outcome. In the military, this type of unprincipled demand or request is referred to as an unlawful order. That is an order that is either illegal, immoral, and/or unethical, and any military member given such an order is not obligated to follow it. I am not naive in my thinking that in every situation, your boss or supervisor will be understanding of your noncompliance, see the wrongness in what they have requested of you, and will willingly stand down or retract the directive. In some situations where there is defiance to a command, things could turn contentious even to the point of you losing your job or position because of your willful disobedience in the mind of your boss or supervisor. This can be difficult to accept at any level. Despite the degree of difficulty, if God led you to that position or job, then He can lead you to another one that might be much better. In fact, in some instances, that whole situation just might be a God-given test (sort of like Job's experience), and He is waiting to reward you with a better position or job. Perhaps it may be that you needed to learn certain lessons in the current position that will be needed for the next position or the next step in God's masterful plan for your life and that He's ready to promote you to that next endeavor. This is some real championship stuff.

Now that my preface is completed, here are some of my opinions. If you willfully accept a job or position with a full understanding and scope with all the expected responsibilities, pertinent logistics, and policies of the job/position explained prior to the commencement of employment, then it's expected of you by God and the employer to always put forth nothing less than your best effort. Anything less than that is spiritually and carnally fraudulent. No excuses. Proverbs 18:9 states that "one who is slack in his work is brother to one who destroys." If you feel deserving of a raise in pay and/or promotion, then I admonish you to schedule an appointment with your supervisor, human resource representative, or employer designee to express your sentiment. If you both agree, congratulations!

You've successfully accomplished your mission. If there's push-back or disagreement from the employer or representative, then you, of course, have the option of either promptly planning an exit strategy or remaining in your current position. Before finalizing your decision, first and foremost, I strongly recommend that you seek God via prayer to ascertain His will for you concerning the situation. If you are to stay with the respective company or business, it is incumbent upon you to give your best daily regardless of antithetical feelings presumably possessed as a result of being turned down for the promotion or pay raise. Admittedly, this would be very difficult to do in your own strength; thus, it would definitely require you to petition our heavenly father through prayer to give you strength daily to accomplish this feat.

If you are in a toxic work environment or a less-than-optimal work setting and are frequently being disrespected, then, of course, it would be very difficult to optimally perform in this stringent or harsh environment. The Lord does not expect nor does he desire for us to be treated like a doormat or an old dishrag. We are God's elect, His chosen people holy and dearly loved (Colossians 3:12). In situations like these, I strongly urge you to pray and ask God what your next step is according to His plan and how you are to mitigate situations.

Love and Respect Others to the Best of Your Ability

This speaks to the heart of Christianity. Jesus said in Matthew 22:39, "Love your neighbor as yourself." Contextually, He stated that this was the second greatest commandment with the first being, "Love the Lord your God with all your heart and with all your soul and with all your mind" (Matthew 22:37–38).

We are commanded by God to love others, period. That is our second most important directive that we as Christians were given and expected to live by. It is imperative that we love people despite their faults, flaws, shortcomings, idiosyncrasies, mistakes, sins (recent and remote), sexual orientation, race, creed, nationality, or religion. Yes, I did include religion. We are commanded to love without any stipulations or conditions. We must be careful not to allow our differences in opinions, views, or beliefs to tarnish our thoughts and corrode our hearts where we become disparaging to those who oppose our beliefs. Let me be abundantly clear here. I am not suggesting nor implying that we in any way compromise our morals, values, standards, or beliefs. We should never do that. But what I am saying is that we should not castigate or ostracize those who hold differing views, beliefs, or opinions from ours. I strongly believe that our rock-solid, unwavering demonstration of love and Christlike attributes with God's touch may be the precise formula that wins the lost over to God or proselytize those of other faiths or religions. We should be slow to prejudge, judge, stereotype, or criticize others based on their appearances or actions. Instead, learn and/or seek to understand their backstory first before formalizing opinions about them. For example, (I have heard this occurring a time or two in churches of different denominations) a visitor enters a church for the first time, and if he or she appears disheveled or unkempt or discovered to have dressed inappropriately, they are instantaneously judged, talked about, given the cold shoulder, and in some cases scorned then asked to leave the house of God. In many cases, we are quick to cast judgment or a scathing rebuke about someone without understanding their backstory. Remember, friends, Jesus said, "Come as you are." Ideally, a person with a peculiar appearance should first be cordially approached and then taken aside privately, preferably by a designated church representative or official, and their current situation, as well as their spiritual condition, should be discussed in an earnest attempt to ascertain the person's backstory.

Another example of a situation that is familiar to me is when a person has been ostracized or scorned for committing a known sin and is vilified or demonized by the church for reasons such as abortion, divorce, or pregnancy out of wedlock. Now, I realize these are hot-button issues among believers, and I want to be crystal clear here about my stance on them. I believe, biblically, they are all wrong because they run contrary to God's views. However, they are not sins that cannot be forgiven by God despite human opinion. Jesus touted in Mark 3:28–29 that the only sin that is unforgivable is blasphemy against the Holy Spirit. However, persons considering such serious irreversible or irrevocable acts should understand the extreme magnitude and grave consequences that would result from making such life-altering decisions. In the case of abortion, I am not talking about a situation where a woman gets pregnant as result of a rape or an incestuous relationship because those are very difficult, sensitive situations that require intense prayer and, potentially, Christian counseling. I am referring to an aborted pregnancy as a result of sexual intercourse between two mature, consenting adults. I very much oppose abortion in these situations. All sin is detestable in the eyes of the Lord, but there isn't a God-ordained, codified system of ranking sins; they all stink equally to Him. However, our heavenly Father is willing to forgive us for committed sins if we confess our sins and repent with a contrite heart and earnestly reconcile in our hearts not to commit that sin or those sins again. Therefore, if our Father loves us so much that He sent Jesus Christ to die on the cross for our sins and Jesus loved us so much that He gave up His life in the most demonstrated act of agape (unconditional) love and forgiveness, then who are we not to forgive?

Although I referenced abortion here, divorce or other sins thought to be abominable can be referenced in the same manner.

COMMAND OF GODLY CHAMPIONSHIP

T he expected leadership role that accompanies that of a godly champion is vital to God's movement to win hearts on earth. We are all called to be God's spiritual leaders, and the preferred leadership style is that of a servant leader. This type of leadership was modeled by Jesus Christ. Jesus states in Matthew 20:25–28: "Oh know that the rulers of the Gentiles lord it over them, and their high officials exercise authority over them. Not so with you, instead, whoever wants to become great among you must be first your servant, and whoever wants to be first must be your slave just as the Son of Man did not come to be served, but to serve, and to give His life as a ransom for many." Servant leadership is not about the leader basking in the glory of accolades received from subordinates and admirers. Nor is it about the leader pompously walking around bragging about the leadership position(s) held. It is all about God's divine plan, His people who He strategically places under us to serve, and His mission, which is to affect His will on earth to advance His kingdom. We must be careful to guard our hearts and minds against the subtle infiltration and pervasiveness of pride, which can totally shipwreck the divine purposes of God in our lives, potentially resulting in the perversion of our destiny and the destruction of His intended will in the earth. Pride is an old but very powerful tool used by Satan to divert our attention and focus away from God and directs it onto ourselves, thereby driving a wedge between God and us resulting in God's perfect plans thwarted. Pride causes tremendous, and in some cases, irreparable damage. Pride disables us, rendering us powerless and ineffective in the hands of God. We see in Proverbs 16:18 that "pride goes before destruction, a haughty spirit before a fall," and in Proverbs 18:12, "Before a downfall the heart is proud, but humility comes before honor." Dr. Charles F. Stanley states in his book, *Landmines in the Path of the Believer*, "of all the struggles discussed in this book, pride is the one that has the most devastating results. Many of our problems result from pride's destructive work in our lives, but unfortunately, too many people fail to realize this. They become prideful over the good things God has given them—jobs, families, children, churches, pastors, education, neighborhoods, and much more." Pastor Stanley further touts how God despises pride and arrogance. Proverbs 8:13 states, "I hate pride and arrogance, evil behavior, and perverse speech." Pride is kryptonite in our lives as godly champions. It is the antithesis of humility. Humility gives rise to honor; pride breeds arrogance and conceit resulting in self-destruction. Pride is often subtle. It can slowly and stealthily infiltrate our hearts, contaminating our hearts, minds, and souls over time and culminating in a fall from grace. Consequentially, we undergo a God-directed spiritual time-out. We're placed on a shelf as an act of God's loving discipline so that we can become refined, reshaped, remolded, and purified to remove the stink of pride so that we can re-enter the race for Him again in His timing. Frequently, God will use brokenness as the vehicle by which this process is achieved.

The triumphant and tragic story of King Saul comes to mind when discussing the issue of pride. King Saul was Israel's first and long-awaited king whose life was tragically and sadly ended in a horrendous death because of the overwhelming pride, jealously, envy, and disobedience that had gradually developed in his life. I encourage you, if you do not already know the story of King Saul or if you need to be refreshed, read 1 Samuel 8–15.

CHAPTER 4

DON'T DIE TO THE SOUP

This is simply reflective of the biblical story of twin brothers Jacob and Esau (Genesis 25:19–34). Jacob, the younger of the two, is described more or less as a mama's boy who stayed in the tents (home), loved by his mother Rebekah. Esau, the older of the two, is described as an outdoorsman and a skillful hunter loved by his father Isaac. One day while at home, Jacob was cooking a pot of stew. Esau, upon returning home from hunting, felt famished and asked Jacob for some of his stew. Jacob stipulated to Esau that he could have some stew only if he sells his birthright to him. The birthright was an inherited blessing typically bestowed upon the oldest son by his father. This was a super big deal in the Jewish culture because the father was ceremoniously acknowledging his son before God so that God's hand may be upon him for a fruitful and prosperous future. At that moment, Esau felt famished and desperate for food. He stated, "What good would my birthright do me if I die from hunger?" Thus, he agreed to relinquish his birthright to his brother Jacob for a bowl of stew (soup). Looking at this story at first glance, you may think how stupid it is to give up valuable future blessings for a simple bowl of soup. However, his relentless desire to satisfy an intense, acute desire of the flesh unfortunately led to a poorly made decision that would regrettably and profoundly impact his life forever. In essence, he was truly shortsighted. He forfeited a huge eternal blessing for a short-term, carnal desire. Unthinkable? Maybe, but we make some of those same unfortunate decisions today. We "die to the soup" when we commit adultery or participate in promiscuous activity at any level, unscrupulously indulge in shady business deals, or lie and/or cheat in our relationships to get ahead in the corporate world or school. When we do these things, we rob ourselves of the bountiful blessings and forfeit the prosperity that God has in store for us. Furthermore, we commit idolatry when we devote our heart's attention to something above and beyond the degree of which we devote to our Lord. God has stated that He is a jealous God and despises it when we divert our devoted attention away from Him to someone or something else. Satan's game plan is to disqualify God's sacred people from the race God has authorized us to run to advance His kingdom and reflect His glory. Satan will shipwreck our lives, service, and calling by causing confusion, contention, and disorder to inspire ill-advised, disadvantageous decisions. Do not die to the soup! We must remain steadfast to God's purpose, plan, and will for our lives and keep our feet firmly planted/fixed to the path that He has carved out for our lives.

CHAPTER 5

GRASSHOPPER MENTALITY

Prior to crossing over the Jordan River into Canaan, the promised land, God ordered Moses to send men to spy out the promised land. Let me give the brief backstory for all who may not be familiar with history. The enslaved Israelites endured several years of cruelty at the hands of their captors, the Egyptians. God directed Moses to go to Egypt to champion the release of the Israelites from captivity. Moses obeyed and successfully led the mass exodus of Israelites out of Egypt per God's instruction. En route to Canaan, the promised land, God demonstrated His presence with Israel by miraculously parting the Red Sea as a pathway of escape. Prior to entering the promised land, the Israelites had to pass through a vast stretch of wilderness. Upon receiving God's directive, Moses sent twelve men, including mighty warriors Joshua and Caleb, to spy out the promised land and report to Moses and Israel their findings. They reported that the land flowed with milk and honey as a symbol of its fruitfulness and prosperity. They brought back ripe fruit as a sign that the land can provide good food for sustenance. However, ten out of the twelve men, excluding Joshua and Caleb, had a defeatist perspective because they viewed the inhabitants of the land as unconquerable. They reported to Moses and the Israelite community that the people in the land were giants stronger than they were and that they (the Israelites) appeared like "grasshoppers" in the eyes of the Canaanites. Recall that this was the land God promised the Israelites, and He gave them strict instruction to conquer all inhabitants then subdue the land. It was discovered to be flowing with milk and honey, which was emblematic of the prosperity and richness of the land. However, instead of focusing on the promise of God, the ten Israelites abandoned the promise of God and chose to focus on the perceived problem in front of them. Interestingly enough, the Bible doesn't state how the Canaanites perceived the Israelites, but the Israelites perceived themselves as inferior, inadequate, and hopeless. As a result of the report given by the ten faithless men, the Israelite community began to rail and rebel against Moses, Moses's brother Aaron, and God. They actually said among each other, "If only we had died in Egypt or in the desert. Let's choose a leader and go back to Egypt." Wow! That's incredible because the Israelites were enslaved and treated very harshly by the Egyptians for four hundred years or more; thus, Egypt represented slavery, bondage, and very harsh treatment to the Israelites. Why would they want to return to that? Why would they want to return to the rigors of slavery, beatings, and cruel, inhumane treatment instead of stepping out on faith and believing what God told them in regard to obtaining the promised land? They had already witnessed one of the most profound miracles performed by God, the parting of the Red Sea, as part of God's guarded path and freedom walk for the Israelites in their mass exodus from Egypt. I believe it was due to familiarity and fear of the unknown. They were familiar with the ways of the Egyptians, and they knew just what to expect from them (food and other provisions) despite suffering abject cruelty. They were consumed by their fear of a presumed, unfavorable outcome as a result of the potential battle for the promised land, and it outweighed and superseded their belief, trust, and faith in what God told them. They focused on the perceived problem and lost focus on the promise spoken by the almighty God Himself. So they would much rather submit to the bondage of slavery and suffer abuse and maltreatment than embrace the truth spoken by the almighty God and walk in the success that He had already set in motion. As a result of their unbelief and lack of trust, all Israelites twenty years old and older who grumbled against the Lord perished in the desert and never experienced the joys of living in the promised land. However, Joshua and Caleb successfully crossed over into the promised land and reaped the benefits God had promised them.

It is important to note that God never desired for any of the Israelites to see themselves anything less than a conqueror. That same desire still holds true today for those of us who are true believers. The apostle Paul proclaimed that "we're more than conquerors in Christ Jesus" (Romans 8:37). We are the children of God Most High, blessed with the indwelling of the Holy Spirit who gives us the power to successfully overcome any situation. The intimidated Israelites were consumed by the perceived insurmountable problem at hand instead of centering their focus on the problem solver who had already yielded the victory over the natives. We tend to do the same today. When facing perceived insurmountable odds or obstacles, sometimes we shift our focus away from the Problem Solver (God) and allow ourselves to be overwhelmed by the problem at hand. During tumultuous times, we could potentially get so overwhelmed by the circumstances that we forget the promises of God (i.e., being more than conquerors). God has purchased us with a monumental price paid by the blood of Christ. Therefore, in Christ we are ahead, not behind, greater than, never less than, always the head and not the tail, and above, not beneath. Godly champions are true leaders, not followers. We are victors!

CHAPTER 6

FRUIT FOR THOUGHT

We, as people, are recognized by the fruit that we bear according to Matthew 7:16-20. Below are the perspectives of my wife and me regarding the manifestation of fruit that we bear.

The outward expression of our personality is shaped keenly by our character. Our conduct, communication style (both verbal & non-verbal), actions, and reactions reflect the content of our character which is the proverbial "heart of a person". The attributes of our character can also be defined figuratively as fruit. The fruit we exhibit or manifest to the world will either reflect our sinful nature commonly referred to as our flesh or our spiritual nature. The fruit of our sinful nature as listed in Galatians 5:19-21 and Col 3:5: sexual immorality, lust, evil desires, greed, idolatry, impurity, debauchery, witchcraft, hatred, discord, jealousy, fits of rage, selfish ambition, dissensions, envy, drunkenness, orgies, and the like. I will also personally add lying, cheating, deception, conceit, arrogance, covetousness, and killing. The fruit of the Spirit as listed in Galatians 5:22 & 23: love, joy, peace, forbearance (patience), kindness, goodness, faithfulness, gentleness, and self-control. When we walk according to our flesh or sinful nature instead of by the Holy Spirit, we seek to gratify the selfish desires and ego-inflating characteristics that promote self-righteous behavior. When we walk according to the Holy Spirit instead of our flesh, our thoughts, and actions are inspired out of wisdom, love, prudence, discernment, discretion, and compassion. There is a strong sense of connection to God and a heavenly understanding which translates into acts of love, joy, humility, kindness, and promotion of peace, which allows for benevolent service resulting in personal fulfillment beyond earthly pleasures.

When a particular seed is planted in fertile soil, irrigated, and cultivated, the expectation is for it to eventually produce a tree that will produce nothing less than ripe, delicious fruit. If the seed is from good stock, it will produce good fruit. However, if the seed is from bad stock or is tainted then bad fruit will result. The fruit produced will ultimately reflect the quality of the seed planted. A good seed cannot produce a tree that will render bad fruit. Conversely, A bad seed cannot produce a tree that will render good fruit. God has planted his awesome seed within us, the Holy Spirit. He cultivates us with His Word and expects us (the figurative trees) to bear the excellent fruit reflective of the exceptional quality of His Spirit. Luke 6:43-45 states that "No good tree bears bad fruit, nor does a bad tree bear good fruit. Each tree is recognized by its fruit. People don't pick figs from thornbushes, or grapes from briers. A good man brings out of the good stored up in his heart, and an evil man brings evil things out of the evil stored up in his heart. For the mouth speaks what the heart is full of." 3 John 1:11 states "Dear friend, do not imitate what is evil but what is good. Anyone who does what is good is from God. Anyone who does what is evil has not seen God." Jesus makes it quite clear that the outward expressions of our character will identify us as good or bad, no in-between. Unmistakenly, People who express and promote love, peace, compassion, empathy, and unity bear good fruit. However, people who spue vitriolic rhetoric, promote violence, and division, are purveyors of hatred towards others and bear bad fruit. We will be remembered for the fruit we bear. It is imperative for us to keep in mind that what we say, and how we communicate and interact with others will speak volumes about the type of fruit that we bear. As Godly Champions and ambassadors of Christ, we are expected by God to always bear good fruit in every circumstance, interaction, or situation so that the effectiveness of our testimony and our ability to spread the gospel is not impaired. Love and faithfulness matter the most to God. Unconditional love for him and unwavering faith in him along with genuine, enduring love for people touches the heart of God. We represent God's championship DNA when we love him, love people, and effectively spread his gospel to others.

H. Wesley Dykes, Jr.

Each morning, as you awaken and find comfort in the tranquility of your home, take a moment to pray. With every prayer, you will sense the presence of God's Spirit enveloping your heart, igniting a profound joy that cannot be attributed to worldly circumstances. The Spirit of God is present and prepared to guide you, just as He has guided us. There exists a path to live with peace, patience, and joy. When your heart is brimming with God's love, you will recognize that your journey is ongoing. His love has the power to transform our hearts. You will discover a new path abundant with fruit that has the potential to transform not only your life but also the lives of those around you. Despite adversities you have encountered such as the loss of loved ones, struggles with illness, and various challenges, there remains a light within you that appears to endure unwaveringly. You may grapple with inquiries regarding your purpose and self-worth. However, as a child of God, you rely on the assurance provided by the Holy Spirit, which grants you a peace that transcends understanding. There exists a profound power within you that may remain beyond your full comprehension. It may feel like an unseen force, gentle yet compelling, guiding you with every step. You may have heard tales of the spirit of God, a presence that permeates all living beings, reaching the hearts of those who have faith. It manifests as a flame of love and wisdom, capable of illuminating even the darkest moments. For the first time, you may sense the spirit of God moving within you like a gentle breeze, stirring your heart. The spirit is not merely an abstract idea or a distant entity; it is a living force within you, integral to your very existence. It provides the strength you need to navigate challenging times. God, being a spirit, is not a figure you can see, yet He is something you can feel in every part of your being. As you begin to experience His divine presence more profoundly, it will influence your decisions, fill you with compassion for those in distress, and grant you courage in the face of fear. God imparts wisdom via the Holy Spirit during moments of uncertainty, and love flows from you in unforeseen ways. You become an outlet for God's presence in the world, and with each step you take, you come to realize that you are never alone. You should consistently exhibit a kind-hearted disposition and be recognized for your gentle spirit and profound faith in God. Always approach others with compassion and empathy. Each day, through every small gesture of love, patience, or kindness, God nurtures the Fruit of the Spirit within your heart. The fruit you possess is not solely for your benefit; it is also meant to be shared with others. When you share it, it will multiply. Always offer words of hope and strength to those who are suffering and fearful. The spirit of God will work through you, endowing you with an inexplicable clarity and understanding for others. As the spirit of God moves within the hearts of believers, it galvanizes the courage and unity necessary to overcome challenges, making the journey more sustainable. When we walk in harmony with his Spirit, we manifest the fruits of the Holy Spirit. These fruits symbolize the attributes that the Holy Spirit fosters within us. I will illustrate the fruits that God wishes to cultivate in our lives. The foremost of these is love, which serves as the cornerstone of all fruits. God's love unites us, even in moments of division or misunderstanding. Joy follows a faith that remains unshaken by circumstances. This joy arises from the assurance that God is always with us, regardless of the challenges we encounter. When we recognize the love of the Creator of the universe, joy becomes an enduring presence in our lives. Next is peace, a peace that transcends human understanding. It is not derived from external conditions but stems from the knowledge that God is sovereign. This peace soothes our hearts amidst the turmoil surrounding us. Patience emerges after peace, as the Spirit empowers us to withstand trials without losing our composure or faith in God. We learn to wait with hope, confident in His unwavering faithfulness. Other virtues include kindness, goodness, faithfulness, gentleness, and self-control. Each of these qualities mirrors the character of God within us. The Spirit works within us, enabling us to live in a manner that is reflective of the heart of God, worthy of spreading the gospel. Begin with prayer, seeking God to fill you with His Spirit. Each day, strive to walk in His presence despite the urges of the flesh and the temptations of this world. When anger brews and threatens to surface, take a breath, pray for patience and self-control. In moments of despair, seek God earnestly and wholeheartedly and choose joy. When faced with the temptation to act unkindly, select kindness. The Spirit will lead you, and the fruits will gradually flourish within you. Your life will be filled with renewed purpose and profound, lasting joy. The fruits of the Spirit will manifest in your existence, allowing you to witness the transformation that only the Spirit of God can achieve. The influence of God's Spirit is palpable in the lives of those who choose to follow his path. It is a life characterized by love, joy, peace, patience, kindness, goodness, faithfulness, gentleness, and self-control—a life that embodies the heart of God and illuminates the world around them. When one embraces a life characterized by an open heart, consistently striving to serve others and to love them as God loves you, a profound transformation occurs. Recognizing God is the essence of life—acting as the very breath that animates you—enables you to impact the lives of many. This serves as a testament to the divine spirit residing within everyone. It is this same spirit that gently encourages us during moments of stillness, inspiring acts of kindness and instilling a sense of peace within our hearts. This presence is ever ready, awaiting the moment of awakening, prepared to guide us as we navigate the world with love and faith. The concept that the outcomes we produce in the world are indicative of our physical nature or spiritual essence is a fundamental principle in spiritual philosophy. Across various religious and spiritual traditions, the "fruit" of an individual's life is seen as a reflection of their inner character, values, and the journey they undertake.

Misti E. Dykes

GODLY CHAMPION THOUGHTS

I n this chapter, I wanted to provide some godly food for thought that I believe are salient.

One of my more formidable challenges experienced since childhood is eloquent public speaking. I would feel anxious when speaking because my thoughts would flow through my mind faster than I could verbally express them, resulting in stuttering at times. This would occur whether I was speaking corporately in front of a small group or crowd of people or privately during a one-on-one conversation. My anxiety was attributed to a lack of confidence in my ability to articulate my thoughts well. My dearth of confidence stemmed from "stinking thinking" and ignorance of the full power of the Holy Spirit residing within my heart. Despite being well taught about God, Jesus, and the Holy Spirit at an early age by both my family and my local Baptist church, I didn't fully understand or appreciate the enormous power of the Holy Spirit until my walk with Christ began to mature. Recently, during my quiet time while reading the Bible, I came across the passage in 1 Corinthians 1:5–9 whereby Paul is writing to the church of Corinth. It states, "For in him you have been enriched in every way—with all kinds of speech and all knowledge." This passage coupled with Luke 12:11–12 which states, " When you are brought before synagogues, rulers, and authorities, do not worry about how you will defend yourselves or what you will say, for the Holy Spirit will teach you at that time what you should say," reminded me of two salient points: (1) God has anointed me and has already endowed me with the profound, unfettered ability to proficiently organize my thoughts and eloquently articulate them; and (2) the Holy Spirit will alert me to timely, appropriate speech and conversation. This resulted in an enormous confidence boost, which was very much needed. Thus, the anxiety that use to choke out the confidence in my ability to speak had drastically diminished to being nearly nonexistent. As godly champions, we possess the unadulterated, God-given ability to think and speak eloquently, undauntedly, and unabashedly to those who come across our paths to glorify God.

Don't seek the reward. Instead seek the One who gives the reward. Over many years, I worked diligently in everything I did to the seek approval of others, to the likes of parents, teachers, supervisors, fellow physicians, coaches, teammates, and contemporaries. I sought to gain constant public acknowledgment to validate my existence initially as a boy then to feel appreciated as a man. I was extremely focused on receiving awards/rewards (physically/verbally) to substantiate my worth/value. This line of thinking proved to be problematic because of misplacement of focus. I was much more concerned about the thoughts, opinions, and impressions of me formed by others to boost my self-esteem and validate my self-worth rather than the truths that God stated about me as one of His children. As a result of this dysfunctional thinking, my self-confidence and self-esteem waxed and waned, contingent upon the positive or negative perceptions that others had of me. Thus, I found myself in a constant state of emotional flux, a real emotional roller coaster governed by the fickle, outward expressions of others instead of the immutable truth that God has reiterated about me over several years. To break this pernicious cycle of emotional instability, God revealed to me that He alone is my confidence. He reminded me to seek Him first above everyone else and before everything that I set to do so that all will go well for me. He also reminded me that He is my providence, meaning that my successful existence is exclusively predicated on my relationship with Him. Therefore, it was abundantly clear that it is imperative for me to maintain a steady, healthy, daily diet of prayer, Bible reading, worship, faith, and obedience to the beckoning/instruction of the Holy Spirit to encourage an intimate relationship with God.

This is who we are in Christ (NIV):

1. "You're a people holy unto Lord your God" (Deuteronomy 7:6, 14:2).
2. We're His treasured possessions chosen from all people on earth.
3. "As God's chosen people, holy and dearly loved" (Colossians 3:12).
4. "As to come to Him, rejected by humans but chosen by God and precious to Him" (1 Peter 2:4).
5. "Chosen people, Royal Priesthood, a Holy Nation, God's special Possession" (1 Peter 2:9).
6. "We're God handiwork/workmanship, created in Jesus Christ to do good work, which God prepared in advance for us to do" (Ephesians 2:10).
7. "You're not your own; you were bought at a price" (1 Corinthians 6:19–20).
8. "You were bought at a price; do not become slaves of men" (1 Corinthians 7:23).

FINAL THOUGHTS

All humans are masterfully created by the hands of God. However, only those of us who have accepted the Lord Jesus Christ as our undisputed Lord and Savior in whom we place our love, trust, and belief are aptly called His children. It is God's desire for all His children to live routinely as godly champions and to be successful according to His standards by walking in his purpose, plan, and will for which we were created. We are elite and victorious in everything that we are called to accomplish because of our heavenly Father's anointing, appointment, and strength. We are made in His likeness and, thus, have the inherited spiritual gravitas to live, lead, and honor God with fervor. Therefore, as godly champions, let us live life with spiritual gusto and leave everything we have out on the field of life every day for our Lord Jesus Christ!

www.ingramcontent.com/pod-product-compliance
Lightning Source LLC
Chambersburg PA
CBHW051251120626
46547CB00014B/1892